The Poems of
Rowan Williams

The Poems of
Rowan Williams

William B. Eerdmans Publishing Company

Grand Rapids, Michigan / Cambridge, U.K.

© 2002 Rowan Williams

First published 2002 by
The Perpetua Press, Oxford, U.K.

This edition published 2004 in the United States of America by
Wm. B. Eerdmans Publishing Co.
255 Jefferson Ave. S.E., Grand Rapids, Michigan 49503 /
P.O. Box 163, Cambridge CB3 9PU U.K.

Printed in the United States of America

08 07 06 05 04   7 6 5 4 3 2 1

ISBN 0-8028-2685-7

www.eerdmans.com

To the memory of

Anne Ridler

Contents

Foreword, by Phoebe Pettingell   9
Preface   23

Gwen John in Paris   25
Drystone   28
Six O'Clock   29
Our Lady of Vladimir   30
Advent Calendar   31
Return Journey   32
Crossings   33
Déjeuner sur l'Herbe   37
Twelfth Night   38
Great Sabbath   42
Oystermouth Cemetery   45
Third Station   46
Pantocrator: Daphni   47
Augustine   48
Indoors   50
Rublev   51
Snow Fen   52
Kettle's Yard   53
September Birds   54
The White Horse   55
Cornish Waters   56
Bach for the Cello   59
Los Niños   60
First Thing   62
Dream   63
Feofan Grek: the Novgorod Frescoes   64
Thomas Merton: Summer 1966   65
Walsingham: the Holy House   66
Penrhys   67
Curtains for Bosnia   69
Murchison Falls   70
Kampala: the El Shaddai Coffee Bar   71
Woodwind: Kanuga in March   72

REMEMBERING JERUSALEM
Jerusalem Limestone   73
Gethsemane   75
Calvary   76
The Stone of Anointing   76
Easter Eve: Sepulchre   77
Low Sunday: Abu Ghosh   78

GRAVES AND GATES
Rilke's Last Elegy   79
Nietzsche: Twilight   80
Simone Weil at Ashford   81
Tolstoy at Astapovo   82
Bereavements   83
Winterreise   84
Flight Path   86
Ceibr: Cliffs   87
Windsor Road Chapel   88
Deathship   89

CELTIA
Gundestrup: The Horned God   90
The Sky Falling   91
Posidonius and the Druid   93
Altar to the Mothers   94

TRANSLATIONS
Experiencing Death (Rilke)   95
Roundabout, Jardin du Luxembourg   96
Angel   97
Hymn for the Mercy Seat (Ann Griffiths)   98
I Saw him Standing   100
Strata Florida (T. Gwynn Jones)   101
Song for a Bomb (Waldo Williams)   102
In the Days of Caesar   103
After Silent Centuries   104
Die Bibelforscher   106
Between Two Fields   107
Angharad   110

Foreword

"Seeings and Readings": The Poems of Rowan Williams

Normally, the appointment of a new Archbishop of Canterbury is of little interest to people outside the Anglican Communion — and not necessarily to a percentage of its 80 million members worldwide. However, the choice of Rowan Williams, then Archbishop of Wales, certainly made headlines as soon as it was known that he was on the short list. Why so newsworthy? Well, for one thing, he was the first non-Englishman selected for the Church of England's highest office since the Reformation, and thus a reminder to those of us living outside the British Isles that there is still a difference between Celts like Williams and "Anglo-Saxons." Then there were his shaggy white beard, flying hair and bristly eyebrows, which reminded some commentators of J. R. R. Tolkien's benign wizard, Gandalf. His genial, earthy manner in interviews only added to this impression. The hirsute appearance seemed almost cuddly, which, no doubt, helped inspire "the Rowan Bear" — a bespectacled Teddy in cope and miter (ornamented with a dove to reflect Williams's pacifism) and a cassock "boasting thirty-nine buttons — one for each of the [Church of England's] historic Articles of Religion." No other modern British Churchman would have been the model for a popular toy.

More significantly, however, the new Archbishop is a well-known author, and a controversial one at that. Several twentieth-century English primates were theologians, though Williams's theological work holds its own with the best of theirs; nor is he the first recent church leader to write devotional books. But his audience stretches beyond the churchly with *Lost Icons: Reflections on Cultural Bereavement* — an examination of the emotional impoverishment of contemporary society, and *Writing in the Dust: After September 11* — in which he counseled against revenge. This outspokenness on current issues including human sexuality, no matter how thoughtfully couched, makes him a lightning rod for the kind of attention usually reserved for politicians and pundits.

Most surprisingly, it turns out that Williams is a poet. At the time of his appointment to Canterbury, he had produced two slim volumes of verse. It is so unusual for public figures in the English-speaking world to be poets as well that, I confess, despite long-standing admiration for his prose, my own first reaction was skepticism. Would the poetry turn out to be a hobby, akin to the proverbial "Sunday painting" indulged in by some generals, rock stars, and political leaders? Happily, *The Poems of Rowan Williams* is the genuine article, with a penetrating lyric voice, astonishingly immediate and beguiling. The first two volumes have been combined, with additional new work. Poetic subjects include the paintings of "Gwen John in Paris"; landscapes ranging from the chalky limestone of the hills and gnarled olive trees around Jerusalem or central Africa's "Murchison Falls," to Cambridge fenland, Cornish moors, and the slate-colored sea and cliffs of his native Wales; Russian icons; the monk Thomas Merton fallen passionately in love with a young nurse; the frustration of unconsummated relationships; young women from a "Council Estate" (Britain's odd term for low-income housing projects); "Bach for the Cello"; elegies for parents and friends as well as Tolstoy, Nietzsche, and Simone Weil; ancient Celtic artifacts. Williams has also translated some Rilke and three admired Welsh writers — Ann Griffiths, T. Gwynn Jones, and Waldo Williams.

The appeal of his writing lies in the immediacy of his descriptions. We see at once that this is someone who knows how to really look at things — art, landscapes, emotions — and find the right words to describe what he sees. "Looking hard" at nature, pictures, ideas, and experiences helps us understand not just ourselves, but — more importantly in Williams's view — that which lies outside our subjective self. Finding words and images to convey the effect of something not ourselves expands our capacity to understand and empathize with others, human or otherwise.

Seeing our surroundings accurately is much harder than it sounds. Inevitably, it forces us to confront those aspects we would prefer to filter out — like cruelty, misery, destruction. Williams

does not flinch from the losses, hurts, and sadness that bombard
even everyday existence. "Indoors" concludes:

> This is the house that years built, dropping soil
> from the loose screes. Straddling the hill, the cottage
> > sheds its tiles,
> the books begin to corrugate with damp. Home
> is the cleft where the earth runs, and a little old thin blood,
> home's where the hurt is, white and familiar as a bone.

Most of us have had to relinquish places once central to our emo-
tional being — our "known territory," the site of experiences that
shaped us. Even our memories of them deteriorate with time,
"corrugate with damp." The poet's words seem reluctant, halting,
as if hoping to postpone arrival at this bleak vision of dissolution.
Yet amidst the regret, we feel delight at something so exactly
evoked. Home is, indeed, where the primal "hurt" is, for most of
us: the initial experiences that molded our understanding of de-
privation, not merely our images of comfort and belonging. In the
very moment of empathy with the pain of this poem, enjoyment
is stirred as well. Williams powerfully alludes to this kind of para-
dox in *Writing in the Dust: After September 11* (2002), where he re-
calls struggling out of Trinity Church on Wall Street after the col-
lapse of the first World Trade Tower a few blocks away. The clouds
of dust and debris muffling the streets of Manhattan made the
world seem eerily silent, reminding him of the hushed beauty and
mystery evoked in Robert Frost's "Stopping by Woods on a Snowy
Evening."

Rowan Williams was born in southern Wales on June 14, 1950.
He has lyrically described his natal valley in an interview with *The
Swansea Leader* (November 2002):

> Imagine a great semicircle surrounded by hills, with
> buildings clustered in the middle and one white tower visible
> across the bay, houses creeping up the hills in all directions.
> At night, lights and billows of smoke are seen from the
> steelworks and the power station on the far side and summer

evenings with the sea like glass. From the hills, unexpected views of the Bay as you walk over a crest. A town center still in the Sixties, showing the last signs of war devastation and a not very brilliant post-war rebuilding and a big outdoor market, always crowded and full of strong and wonderful smells.

A severe case of meningitis in infancy left him permanently deaf in one ear and with a limp that persisted throughout childhood. An only child, often kept from school because of illness and unable to participate in certain physical activities, he read in a variety of fields including literature, history, and folklore. The family attended the Presbyterian Church of Wales, but after they moved to Oyster-mouth (a suburb of Swansea) the ten-year-old boy asked his parents to join the local Anglican parish, All Saints. All Saints belonged to the tradition known as Anglo-Catholic. Services combined the rich language of the Book of Common Prayer with music and ritual cho-reography of movement, a worship experience that involves the senses as well as the intellect. For Anglo-Catholics, the veil between the visible and invisible realms frequently becomes gauzy. Time and eternity, the living and dead, divine and human all seem to meet at a central point of the eucharist. This sense of the conjunction of tem-poral and eternal pervades much of Williams's writing.

Anglo-Catholics are not monochrome. Though their ethos about the importance of ritual in worship remains constant, opin-ions, even theology, can vary widely. The strain of Anglo-Catholi-cism that captivated the future poet and Archbishop cares deeply about social justice and the radical equality of God's concern for people regardless of their condition or place in the world's pecking order. Williams's poems brim with compassion: for the weak, marginalized and outcast, even the powerful who "know not what they do." Several touch on the sufferings caused by civil wars in the Balkans. In "Penrhys" — where a modern "council estate" has been constructed on the site of a medieval shrine to the Madonna — he sees in the "thin teenage mothers by the bus stop," standing in the rain smoking and wisecracking while their babies squall, a kinship with the gaunt gothic statue of Mary. We recall that she, too, must have been very young (and unwed) when she became pregnant. Suffering is never far from Williams's perceptions. In

"Twelfth Night," the Magi experience anxiety and disappointment that the child they have come to worship is, after all, human. He, too, must suffer and die, though before that Herod will order many other children to be slaughtered. How could humanity not hope this "newborn king" heralded a return to the innocence of Eden, an end to misery, a return to fearless childhood when everything felt safe? But, as Williams preached in his 2002 Christmas meditation, for all the progress of two thousand years of history, "still the innocent are killed."

> Behind the stars no happy end,
> no dissolution of our scars,
> no garden plot, no spilling grass:
> the cot is empty.
>
> Where has the child gone, to what fire,
> what rubbish bin, what coins were laid
> to close his eyes? give us at least
> the choice of sending flowers.

The mystery of the Incarnation does not repudiate suffering but encompasses it in the divine nature. When the Child Christ finally answers the Wise Men's questions, his voice carries the same authority with which God addressed Job. The divine response to our suffering is the promise that God understands our pain, which has some purpose in the heavenly scheme of things:

> You still are children, innocence not gone,
> what memory of yours is worth the name?
> where were you when the world's foundations
> set in children's blood?
>
> You still are children; all that you have known
> is fear, not guilt, have felt the blade,
> but not the handle of the moulder's knife
> carving a mind.
>
> Your histories belong to me; here is
> not innocence but absolution, for

your scars are true, but I (always)
will bleed in them.

Your memories belong to me; I lie
awake at night and see for ever, while
the stars shall fall like leaves
to cover you.

The poets Williams has named as his particular early influ-
ences — T. S. Eliot, W. H. Auden (whose work made him realize
"how disciplined you had to be to write"), and Geoffrey Hill —
all modeled the search for a kind of language that could ade-
quately express the human anguish of poverty, nihilism, ill-
ness, atrocities, the kind of misery that, too often, societies try
to shut out or deny. Although it took Williams years to find the
metaphorical language to express these ideas so eloquently,
people who knew him back in his student days already noticed
his compassion. At Christ College, Cambridge, where he studied
theology, he took tramps into his rooms when they had no
place else to sleep.

Already attracted to the theology of Eastern Orthodox
churches, he pursued this interest at Oxford for his postgraduate
studies in 1971-72. Many of his poems reflect the ethos of Ortho-
doxy — especially in describing icons like "Our Lady of Vladimir"
or the mosaic dome depicting the great "Pantocrator: Daphni,"
"Feofan Grek: The Novgorod Frescoes," and "Rublev" — the four-
teenth-century Russian icon painter. This last poem has the artist
relate how

One day, God walked in, pale from the grey steppe,
slit-eyed against the wind, and stopped,
said, Colour me, breathe your blood into my mouth.

I said, Here is the blood of all our people,
these are their bruises, blue and purple,
gold, brown, and pale green wash of death.

These (god) are the chromatic pains of flesh,
I said, I trust I make you blush.

Like Jacob at Peniel, Rublev wrestles with his Creator to win a blessing.

Williams briefly flirted with the idea of entering a religious order — he was especially drawn to the Roman Catholic Benedictine tradition. The poems, however, reveal ambivalence about celibacy in their attraction to women. In "Crossings," a sequence of eight sonnets, a man teeters on the verge of a romantic relationship. A mixture of sexual excitement, apprehension, fear of rejection, and frustration keeps him from spilling over into a declaration. The speaker finds himself hampered by both his ability to imagine what the woman might be thinking and his scruples about making the situation more awkward than it already is. Under such circumstances there can be no consummation. In the end, he queries ironically, "So did we ever have an assignation/ Under the station clock?" exploiting the romantic convention beloved of movies and plays in which lovers "might have snatched a word." Instead,

You never came, we both of us could say,
Angry, relieved, rejected, gone away.

After completing his doctorate in philosophy in 1975, Williams went to teach at Mirfield Theological College run by the Community of the Resurrection, an influential Anglican religious order. He was ordained to the priesthood in 1978 — by which time he had been appointed tutor at Westcott House, Cambridge. His academic career advanced rapidly through a number of positions at Cambridge and then, from 1986 through 1992, as Lady Margaret Professor of Divinity at Oxford. In 1981, he married Jane Williams. Throughout those years, he wrote and published four books on spirituality and theology as well as a much-reprinted collection of sermons, *Open to Judgment* (called *A Ray of Darkness* in the American edition). He also brought out his first volume of poems, *After Silent Centuries* (1984). The work from this period demonstrates a progressive fluidity of expression. He becomes adept at making points real to his audience. In particular, the poetry he wrote at the time displays what he calls "the slow coming to the boil of metaphors and phrases" that comes to meaning through a concentrated image, as with this description of the bleak, flat Cambridge landscape in winter:

> Sketches of street and hedge
> and scribbled farms, the pencilled query notes
> against the ledger, smear down steadily
> to a grey page, rinsed at last
> to its sharp grain again.
>
> ("Snow Fen")

Here, the academic world of the university so pervades the landscape that it transforms an "academic sky" into a writing tablet.

Williams did not confine himself to intellectual and literary endeavors in these years. He chose to work in a parish, living for a while in the curate's residence among the poor. He subsequently served at Leicester Cathedral and at Christ Church, Oxford. He was elected Bishop of Monmouth in 1991, and in 1999 became Archbishop of Wales. Williams's second volume of verse, *Remembering Jerusalem*, came out in 2001 along with a spate of prose works — on politics, spirituality, and theology. His short book *Writing in the Dust: After September 11* brought him a wider audience. Some of the poems from the second collection reflect the experiences of the Episcopal office. "First Things" hints at the hate mail public persons receive, while "Dream" suggests the anxiety of having to work with intractable situations, the fear that mistakes will box one in where "there is no corner/left to turn." On February 27, 2003, Rowan Williams was enthroned Archbishop of Canterbury. He had chosen the date because it is the Feast of George Herbert, England's foremost devotional poet, whose compassionate humility and openness to human frailty shape his own "seeing and readings."

Williams's verses bristle with insights. "Gwen John in Paris" — the work that begins this volume — is spoken in the voice of the sister of the Welsh painter, Augustus John. An artist herself, she also modeled for Rodin, with whom she had an affair. When the poet has her call herself "Mrs. Noah" and refer to her "clothes-peg head," someone familiar with the paintings will picture the self-portraits in which her small round head with the hair tightly pulled back looks exactly like an old-fashioned clothespin, not to

mention the peg figures turned on a dowel that often people a
child's toy ark. Gwen John's love of animals, which she often
drew, also makes her a fitting "Mrs. Noah." The evocative pictures
she made of her Paris garret radiate self-contained stillness, but,
as Williams observes, they also pulsate with quiet tension:

> Afternoon light
> swells like a thundercloud in the attic, busy
> around an empty chair, draped like the dead king's throne.

The dead king refers to the absent Rodin, but may also refer to
Christ, as the artist became a devout Catholic. Gwen John later
made sketches based on family photographs of Thérèse of Lisieux.
The poem links the teenage saint's renunciation of self-will with
the artist's hard-won acceptance that her art would achieve less
notice than a man's during her lifetime because when you don't
fit into the expected perceptions of your culture, "you can spend a
short life/not being seen."

The act of "seeing" fascinates Williams. "Gwen John in Paris"
refers to those ways in which each society trains us to overlook
certain people and situations while taking notice of others. But
art is remarkable in the way it allows not just one viewpoint, but a
multiplicity of interpretations. During a philosophical lecture
given in 2002, he observes that "Imaginative construction, verbal
or visual, works to make present an aesthetic object that allows it-
self to be contemplated from a perspective or perspectives other
than those of the artist's own subjectivity. Art makes possible a
variety of seeings or readings." He goes on to argue that it origi-
nates in the ability to understand "the world in this way, a field of
possible readings therefore never reducible to . . . one agenda." In
this way, art differs from much expository writing, especially the
polemical, which hopes to convince everyone of the author's con-
clusion. One vital aspect of compassion is the willingness to ac-
knowledge and accept the difference of another: my recognition
that the next person's existence is as significant as mine. There-
fore, the artist relinquishes possessiveness, permitting a certain
freedom to viewers. At the same time, when we interpret a novel,
poem, or painting, we extend our own perspective to enter into
that of the person who created the work. Williams believes that

secularism undermines "a willingness to see things or persons as the objects of another sensibility other than my own; perhaps also another sensibility other than our own, whoever 'we' are, even if the 'we' is humanity itself." Williams's poetry is always trying to expand the horizons of his "seeings and readings."

"Bach for the Cello" testifies to the profound effect music can have, stirring perceptions beyond the mere sound, in which

> the flesh aches on its string,
> without consummation,
>
> Without loss.

This seems to refer both to the cellist fingering the strings of his instrument and to the way the hearer receives the music as a kind of stasis reminiscent of Keats's Grecian Urn that "dost tease us out of thought/As doth eternity." Williams has said that if he could take only one musical recording to the proverbial desert island, it would be Bach's "Cello Suite Number One in G Major" — obviously the piece described by this poem.

The sequence "Remembering Jerusalem" offers a series of poetic snapshots that, on closer reading, reveal themselves as meditations on several sites of pilgrimage. Those who have visited them will recognize the accuracy of the descriptions. For the rest, they suggest what it must feel like to be there by awakening our senses to the dusty hills "a chalky retching," the twisted shapes of olive trees at Gethsemane, or the way that, when one's hand touches the rock of Calvary, it "comes away/from its complicity moist,/ grimy, sweet-scented." The opening stanza of "Easter Eve: Sepulchre" imagines what the emperor who had it built must have envisioned for this shrine commemorating Christ's tomb:

> Constantine knew, of course, just what he wanted:
> smooth verticals and marble, crushed glass rolled underfoot,
> room for archangels with their orbs and wands,
> space for cool power to stroll relaxed and heavy-footed.

But over the centuries, the building was "folded and packed, crumpled and stripped and boxed" into a mazelike structure full of "corners with don't-ask smells and fairground decorations." While our solipsistic piety might long for the airy grandeur of Constantine's original plan (providing we could be the privileged ones worthy of making our devotions there), the chaotic and tawdry reality, jammed with crying and sweaty people on this holy day, is not inappropriate to worship the Word made Flesh.

Williams's wry, tongue-in-cheek humor comes to the fore in the group of poems entitled "Celtia." Not for him the currently fashionable romance of the ancient Celts' cultural superiority — promulgated in such popular works as Peter Tremayne's "Sister Fidelma" mysteries along with innumerable books in the occult section of bookstores. Instead, the poet muses on the cryptic significance of bronze-age artifacts like the silver Gunderstrup bowl portraying Cernunnos, the horned god, or the remark made by some Celtic chiefs, and owlishly reported by Roman soldiers, that the only thing they feared was that the sky should fall. A Celt himself, Williams guesses the falling sky to be the kind of leg-pull rural people love to practice on foreigners. Once again we are reminded that Williams is not an "English" poet, but Welsh. And, like the hymn writers of his native land who pictured biblical scenes on their own hills, he sometimes transposes action in a similar fashion. "Altar to the Mothers" (referring to the carved stone preserved in the Museum of National Antiquities at Saint-Germain-en-Laye) begins with a lubricious male fantasy of fertility goddesses who are "soft-cheeked and honey-breasted . . . warm thighs," beautiful but with a delicious suggestion of the dominatrix, for spice. Alas for pipe dreams, the actual carving represents three rather dumpy figures muffled in clothing. They remind the poet of a very different kind of woman:

> headscarved and overcoated, waiting for a bus
> to Ebbw Vale or Rotherham; bleak damp endurance of
> the never-up-to-standard world.

These mothers are much more frightening for being the guilt-inducing reality we all know. Shaming us, they intone the time-honored bromides:

Don't think of me. We've always done what seemed the
    right thing
for you, pet. If you don't respect
yourself, no-one will do it for you. If you've got
your health, then there's nothing you can't cope with.
    What time
do you call this? Why aren't you eating?

Which of us wouldn't make sacrifices to try placating this god-
dess, even though we realize we can never find "an up-to-
standard offering" for her? She is the deity of human perfection-
ism, impossible to please, the one who drives us to try becoming
more than human, the spirit that prevents us from acknowledg-
ing our vulnerability.

Paul Tillich defined the difference between a sign and a symbol
by saying that the former merely conveys information while the
latter shares in part the greater reality it points to. Poetry at-
tempts to embody what it describes. It is a kind of incarnation, the
word made flesh. The truth embodied in these particular poems is
that to be human means, at the deepest level, to be most vulnera-
ble. Much of the time, we struggle against that truth. Which of us
wants to admit that we might be less important to others than to
ourselves, not in control of every situation we face, incapable of
fully opening ourselves up to another? Our culture associates vul-
nerability with weaknesses and shame, yet because of our human
vulnerability, God so loved us that he came to earth to experience
suffering and death. The quality that makes Williams's poetry
powerful is his ability to find the words, sometimes lyrical, other
times almost stumbling, that strip experience down to its most
human level. His powerful translation of "Die Bibelforscher: For
the Protestant martyrs of the Third Reich" by the Welsh poet
Waldo Williams proclaims,

Earth is a hard text to read. But what we can be certain of
is that screaming mob is insubstantial mist;
in the clear sky, the thundering assertions fade to nothing.
There the Lamb's song is sung, and what it celebrates
is the apocalypse of a glory
pain lays bare.

This triumphant candor makes us want to read Rowan Williams's poetry so that we may be challenged and enlightened by his "seeings and readings."

Phoebe Pettingell

Preface

This book includes all the poems published in *After Silent Centuries* (1994) and *Remembering Jerusalem* (2001), and some more recent ones.

Several of these pieces began as responses to visual works; in particular, the poems 'Our Lady of Vladimir', 'Pantocrator: Daphni', 'Rublev', and 'Feofan Grek: the Novgorod Frescoes', on some of the best-known and most frequently reproduced images in Eastern Christian art.

Several of the poems are contained in three clusters (clusters rather than sequences, I think, as the order is not of major significance). The first began with a visit to Jerusalem during Orthodox Holy Week in 1995, and makes a fair amount of allusion to the sites and ceremonies of the season; Abu Ghosh is one of the sites traditionally (though not very plausibly) identified with the Emmaus of St Luke's Gospel, scene of the resurrected Jesus' self-disclosure at the end of a journey, when he is recognised as he silently breaks bread. Today, Abu Ghosh is the location of a Benedictine community of French origin.

The 'Graves and Gates' poems reflect a period of several years marked by the death of parents and some close friends, among them the extraordinary figure of Gillian Rose, Jewish philosopher and critic, baptised on the day of her death. Around all this, I found myself thinking about death in general, and about the deaths of some of those I love and admire from a distance as persons and writers; exploring how their deaths uncannily 'metaphorise' something central to their work and thought (Simone Weil's apparent self-starvation, Rilke's throat cancer ...).

'Celtia' embodies a lasting scepticism about some modern romantic pictures of Celtic identity, looking instead at bits of the ancient Celtic world, in the literal form of artefacts from that age and also in the shape of fragments from one or two of the classical writers who describe it.

There are some free translations: three from fairly well-known Rilke poems ('Todes-Erfarhrung', 'Das Karusell' and 'Der Engel', the originals in *Neue Gedichte/New Poems*, translated by Stephen Cohn,

Manchester, Carcanet, 1997, pp. 83, 101, and 67 respectively) and nine from the Welsh.

The versions of poems from Welsh originals require a word of comment. The three writers represented differ widely. Ann Griffiths was a farmer's wife without formal education, who died in 1805, leaving a handful of hymns still remarkable for their bold and extravagant imagery and sustained emotional density. She wrote in conventional eighteenth-century metres, with a straightforward rhyme scheme. She does not employ classical Welsh metrical forms, though she will sometimes use the alliterative idioms typical of these older forms. T. Gwynn Jones (1871–1949) was a major critical and historical writer and, in his time, an innovative poet of high reputation. Waldo Williams (1904–1971) was perhaps the foremost poet of his generation in the Welsh language, a visionary pacifist whose moral and cultural influence was (and is) immense; he was a brilliant exponent of classical Welsh forms, though he could also write in a more 'free' style. The six poems by him which I have translated are taken from *Dail Pren*, Llandysul, Gomer, new edition 1991.

Each of these presents different problems for the translator. A close rendering of poems written in classical Welsh metre can often produce a lifeless English version, because the essential feature, the complex internal assonance and rhyming, disappears. Equally, renderings of poems in metres more recognisable to English readers, like Ann Griffiths' hymns, can soften the odd and 'baroque' quality of the strings of imagery. And to translate one of T. Gwynn Jones' less formally innovative poems in a correspondingly traditional quatrain form does him less than justice. As a result, I have adopted, for all three writers, a style of translation designed to be not at all a literal rendering, but an attempt to re-create the progressions of imagery with something of the energy they have in the original. I hope that to Welsh readers they will still be recognisable; but they are efforts to compose poems in English rather than to give a crib to the Welsh, and I have taken considerable liberties with Ann Griffiths' verse in particular so as to present something appropriately fresh (as she deserves).

For help with these translations, I must gratefully acknowledge the kindness of my friends John Walters and Patrick Thomas. Other friends have helped with comments and reactions over the years, to other pieces here.

ROWAN WILLIAMS

Gwen John in Paris

for Celia

I

I am Mrs Noah: my clothes-peg head
pins sheets out between showers;
in my clean cabin, my neat bed,
the bearded Augusti lumber in and out.

I am Mrs Noah: I call the beasts home
together, the cat to lie down with the slug,
the nun with the flapper. I comb
the hair of ferns to dry on deck.

I am Mrs Noah: arranging the flowers
in bright dust round my garden shed,
I watch the silent sky without doubt,
in the soaked moonlit grass sleep without dread.

I am Mrs Noah: the blossoms in the jug
throw their dense pollen round the stormy room like foam;
my hands hold beasts and friends and light in check
shaping their own thick gauzy rainbow dome.

II

Rodin's fingers : probe, pinch, ease open,
polish, calm. Keep still, he says,
recueille-toi: sit on the rock,
gaze out to sea, and I shall make you
patience on a monument. Keep still.
I kept still; he looked away.

On the stairs. In the yard. I stood,
not noticed, in the middle of half-broken stone,
aborted figures. I was a failed work,

keeping still among the darting birds.
His hand refused to close, my lips
stayed open all hours. He might drop in.

Brushing against Rilke in the corridor:
he smiles with fear or pity. Angels,
polished and black, bump into us
at strange angles. Afternoon light
swells like a thundercloud in the attic, busy
around an empty chair, draped like the dead king's throne.

III [1]

Thérèse dreamed that her father
stood with his head wrapped
in black, lost.

Thérèse looks at the photographer
under his cloth and sees
Papa not seeing her.

I watch Thérèse watching
Papa and wondering when
the cloth comes off.

I watch her thinking
you can spend a short life
not being seen.

Thérèse looks at me and says,
Only when you can't see him do you
know you're there.

She says, Can you see me
not seeing you? That's when
you see me.

[1] Gwen John made numerous sketches from photographs
of St Thérèse of Lisieux as a child.

IV

I sent the boys off with their father.
I shall wait on the drenched hill,
Meudon, my Ararat, where the colours pour
into the lines of a leaf's twist.
And the backs of the chairs and schoolgirls' plaits at Mass
are the drawn discord, expecting
the absolution of light in the last bar.

Drystone

In sooty streams across the hill, rough, bumpy,
contoured in jagging falls and twists, they walk
beyond the crest, beyond the muddy clough,
children's coarse pencil sentences, deep-scored,
staggering across a thick absorbing sheet, dry frontiers
on a wet land, dry streams across wet earth,
coal-dry, soot-dry, carrying the wind's black leavings
from the mill valley, but against the gales
low, subtle, huddling: needs more than wind to scatter them.

There is no glue, there is no mortar subtle,
solid enough for here: only the stained air blowing
up from the brewery through the lean dry gaps;
hard to know how an eye once saw the consonance,
the fit of these unsocial shapes, once saw
each one pressed to the other's frontier, every one
inside the other's edge, and conjured the dry aliens
to run, one sentence scrawled across the sheet,
subtle against the wind, a silent spell, a plot.

Six O'Clock

As the bird
rides up the sky, the last sun
looking up gilds in the hollows
of the wings, an afterthought of gift
to guests ignored and hurt, but no,
the bird rides up the sky, eyes on the night.

When the sun
levels its sights across the grass,
it packs the blades and little animals
so tight, so heavy that you wonder
why they don't tumble over
into their new, uncompromising shadow,
into their inner dark.

Our Lady of Vladimir[1]

Climbs the child, confident,
up over breast, arm, shoulder;
while she, alarmed by his bold thrust
into her face, and the encircling hand,
looks out imploring fearfully
and, O, she cries, from her immeasurable eyes,
O how he clings, see how
he smothers every pore, like the soft
shining mistletoe to my black bark,
she says, I cannot breathe, my eyes
are aching so.

The child has overlaid us in our beds,
we cannot close our eyes,
his weight sits firmly,
fits over heart and lungs,
and choked we turn away
into the window of immeasurable dark
to shake off the insistent pushing warmth;
O how he cleaves, no peace
tonight my lady in your bower,
you, like us, restless with bruised eyes
and waking to

a shining cry on the black bark of sleep.

---

[1] The icon of Our Lady probably dates from the twelfth century,
and is preserved in Moscow.

Advent Calendar

He will come like last leaf's fall.
One night when the November wind
has flayed the trees to bone, and earth
wakes choking on the mould,
the soft shroud's folding.

He will come like frost.
One morning when the shrinking earth
opens on mist, to find itself
arrested in the net
of alien, sword-set beauty.

He will come like dark.
One evening when the bursting red
December sun draws up the sheet
and penny-masks its eye to yield
the star-snowed fields of sky.

He will come, will come,
will come like crying in the night,
like blood, like breaking,
as the earth writhes to toss him free.
He will come like child.

Return Journey

Why are places not neutral?
on the smoky screen of walls,
shop windows, sky and pavement spin
the flickering reels of evidence, dust crawling up
the frames, the privately detected chronicle
of clumsily arranged affairs with time and place.

Grace, yes, but damnation too dissolves
in place, so it is not the future
but the past we know to be incredible,
eluding the imagination: unmoved mover
of uncomprehending souls, shaping the mind
glued to the dusty and unwelcome screen.

Push up the blinds and in the room
nothing has gone, there in the dark
we sit unmovable, the wounds as fresh
as ever, all that was ever done
frozen against the walls in a bright moment,
iron and bitter, bright like life.

Fresh from the freezer, all the smooth pain that settled,
stayed when we went on, sat and nestled,
patiently in the corner, waiting to be collected
when we happen back, it stares in silence
at these new, would-be alien selves,
a still, unsmiling, lifelike face.

Crossings

While I sit mute, suspicious of my choice
(Reserve or fluency), how do I reach
You, then, across the acres of the room?
Yes, all the platitudes are clear enough:
Muteness is eloquence, silence is the stuff
Of sharing, while hands work a busy loom;
But on your flesh my hands will still be blind.
Your face is shut. Your body gives no voice,
But charts a distance. How do we avoid
A treaty with the compromising word?
Knowing that after, when we have destroyed
The ambiguity, the precious surd
Of uncommitted quiet, we shall find
Our honesty still waits to be aligned?

You smiled, apologising for the sound—
The hollow distant penetrating hum
Of a dim underground, fathoms down from us.
In those hard channels silence yields, not here;
Under the crust, a journey's length is clear.
The traveller there has mapped his terminus,
Watches for a predicted stop to come,
Steps in the floodstream, confidently bound
A foreknown distance. I cannot select
Periods so easy from the trodden edge
Of words in flux. Prospects of an unchecked,
Unending bursting into haemorrhage
Cut me a channel where we both, pulled down
Under the hollow humming wheels, shall drown.

Tell me what I am asking, then, what plea
You hear without pronouncing. It is you
Who hold the mirror and who know the name
And will not say it; while the desperate cold
Unchristened infant, years or seconds old,
Tries its new lungs with incoherent blame,
Clench-fisted, begs the necessary clue
That holds the hand of an identity
Its lifelong distance. Absolution's cheap
This way, as I laboriously forget
The guilt of joint conspirators, asleep
Against complaining noises, bodies set
Waiting for one to learn or one to teach:
Casual midwives for miscarrying speech.

Cracks open in the floor across the years.
The rumpled bed of stone shrugs off the heat
Of wooden coverlets, impatient with the dark,
And dust no longer binds the drifting blocks.
How long before the stone has forced the locks?
How long before the flesh has split the bark?
And the foundations, naked to our feet
Carry us stumbling on a bridge that clears
The dust-choked distance? While we wait to see
A waking earth that stirs into the sun,
Our covers still are drawn, the night walks free
Between our frontiers, where no path will run.
Under the wooden shroud, under the stone,
Under the dust, the fields are locked unsown.

The shifting floor, the smeared steps inlaid,
Loosened and footprinted with journey's scars,
Is this a field for growing, this a rock
For building? no: the sedges of a marsh
Where white horizons ring the eyes, and harsh
Bird cry scratches the standing pools, to shock
The marble dark in small and passing stars;
The flats of boring exigence displayed,
Unreckoned distance. This is all I make,
A roofless acting space, a voice exposed
To drop its crying in a careless lake
Of ragged eyes, of watchers undisposed
To see or pity stale romantic scenes
Decent embarrassment clothes with safety screens.

And if I told you, should I be surprised
If you, turning your head, asked me, And why?
The choice is mine, the landscape my design,
The black my painting, and the ice my chill;
Looked bitterly at the evasive skill
That locks me up inside this private sign,
Turning a greedy fascinated eye
On an emotion still uncompromised
At its still distance. If I do not tell,
And play under the bedclothes with conceits,
What prudence keeps me in this glassy cell,
The polished atoms of half-willed defeats?
Well, atoms split, my love, are lovers' death,
Out in the cold, no wind will lend us breath.

To break a lock by giving open tongue,
Stand up, come in and sing us out of doors,
I know stirs recollections in the flesh,
And blows the dust from pictures pushed away.
Collected shadows from another day—
Collected words, packed stinking, tight, unfresh,
Ready to send the shiver down old sores,
Echoes of other bodies, roundly flung
A few year's distance. And the hoarded tears,
Unheard reproaches, wait to be unlocked.
Meanwhile I thoughtfully deploy my fears,
Afraid to find my facile pities mocked,
Afraid my probing taps the blood again,
That my flesh too clouds over with the stain.

So did we ever have an assignation
Under the station clock? an intersection
Of complicated routes? Was there a break
Between connections when we might have snatched a word,
Unusual and hard and timely, stirred
By urgencies too close for us to make
Excuses, plead appointments for protection,
Slew our eyes round, sketch a retreat formation
Into the distance promised by the hiss
And echo of things setting to depart
All round? Eyes scattering far and anxious not to miss
Something or anything; travelling apart.
You never came, we both of us could say,
Angry, relieved, rejected, gone away.

Déjeuner sur l'Herbe

Watching your hands
turn slenderly the glass
I wait for rim to snap
or bowl to spill;
but when it shall
shall there be wine to drop
on the drab summer grass
or only hours' worth of spent sands?

Twelfth Night

In the clean winter pastures of the stars
is innocence, a soft and stinging dark
bathing the cataracted eyes
of age remembering.

In the dry winter chambers of the stars
is infancy, a soul unhistoried,
breathing new air, inheriting
no dead men's speech.

Old men live long between the stars:
where else is virgin earth for minds,
for memories bursting brown skins
and spilling seed?

Old men seek sleep between the stars,
cradles between the thin white fires
to rock away the scars of choice
to a bad dream.

O if we did not know
then we should see the clean stars plain,
through the cool night, forgetting,
should come home.

O if we did not see
then we should know the empty air,
the fields of sheep the fresh and unimagined
scents of spilled grass or leaf.

Now when the stars have called to welcome us,
how shall we not run home?
the far side of the desert promises
tearless childhood,

Now that the stars speak clear to us
the language of our marketplace, and cry
come buy, you poor, for innocence
is cheap tonight.

Journeys for old men are not kind
when comfort's sold to buy the single pearl;
yet the child's eye is lifetime's worth of gold,
world's worth of pilgrimage.

Journeys for old men are not mapped,
but for the backward lodestone of desire
for that oasis where the mind is quenched
under still leaves.

Once in the house we saw the trap:
their eyes told all, the childish mother
nursing the knowing mortal child,
a mocking boy.

Once in the house, the stars smiled back
pleased and sardonic at their wit;
sweet-baited lines that catch unpityingly
in the soft places.

Behind the stars no holiday,
no taking out of recollection, but
a cup pressed full of pasts
incalculable

Behind the stars no happy end,
no dissolution of our scars,
no garden plot, no spilling grass:
the cot is empty.

Where has the child gone, to what fire,
what rubbish bin, what coins were laid
to close his eyes? give us at least
the choice of sending flowers.

Where has the child gone? is the watched sky
a single cenotaph for dead simplicity,
the stars a moss-grown requiescat
in half-remembered alphabets?

And we, conscripted mourners for the funeral,
hands full of soil, left sleepless
with the small corpse, until grey dawn
summons us out?

And we, the prisoners of a narrative
of deaths and soiling, heavy as the world,
of stale and endless air, of age,
scents of senility?

The child says, True, this market does not sell
forgetfulness. In a still pool
I hold a glass to all your storms,
to all your eyes.

The child says, True, for nothing is undone
beyond the stars, the tree that grows tonight
is hung with all the lives of men and women,
all your deaths.

You still are children, innocence not gone,
what memory of yours is worth the name?
where were you when the world's foundations
set in children's blood?

You still are children; all that you have known
is fear, not guilt, have felt the blade,
but not the handle of the moulder's knife
carving a mind.

Your histories belong to me here; here is
not innocence but absolution, for
your scars are true, but I (always)
will bleed in them.

Your memories belong to me; I lie
awake at night and see for ever, while
the stars shall fall like leaves
to cover you.

Great Sabbath

Unwatched, the seventh dawn spreads,
Light smoothing out the sky, firm hands
Smearing a damp clay horizon-wide.
They wake , then lie unsurely side by side,
Knowing the ache and pull of novel bands,
The night's new memories grinding in their heads,

Not understood, their bodies newly strange.
Outside, the new light soaks the ground;
They chill, turn in towards each other's heat,
Then roll apart to test uncertain feet
On unknown earth. The dripping dawn around
Confirms the unformed fear. The world can change.

Outside an absence. While they learned and slept,
It had drawn off behind the sky's stone face.
The world between their bodies and their palms
Is left to turn. The silence calms.
The morning's news is plain; the centre space
Is empty. Under the trees where he once stepped

It is for you to go. Under the gaping sky
You wake, he sleeps, you make, he lies at rest.
He will not come again; last night you made
A future he will not invade.
Today the sun is buried, unexpressed;
You shall shape how to live and how to die.

You shall make change. He leaves no room
For his own hand; you shall be history,
You shall build heaven, you shall quarry hell.
No one shall say you have (or not) made well.

And, bored and pious, talk of mystery,
When weeds are choking up his tomb.

We make, he sleeps. Only his bloody dreams
Tell him the works of freedom on the earth.
Your liberty his flight, your future and his death.
He dreams your hell for you to draw your breath,
Out of his emptiness he lets your birth,
It is his silence echoes back the screams.

For they have not forgotten everything;
They wake and lie unsurely side by side
And listen to a laboured, steady breath,
Insistent, unconsoled, remembered death.
A small-hours passing on the turning tide,
Alone and never taught what key to sing.

He will not come again, not in the form
He walked on your first earth. But will you know
Him when he slips, a dosser, through the door?
Oh yes. Who else will touch the raw
Salt, unhealed memory of worlds ago,
Whispering, once you knew, once you were warm.

Listen for promises, fantasize for care,
And you will fill the neutral sky with lead,
Make chains to stop the quiet flow of chance,
Sell all your working for a stripper's dance.
He chose his death; why can he not be dead,
And leave the bloody dreams at home elsewhere?

Drink up your tears; you can no longer need
The luxury of an old, cheap compassion.
To bury him may be heavy cost,
But buys our future when today is lost,

Buys the clean stone from which we can refashion
Our image sorted by his remembered greed.

He asks his present back; the clay-daubed hands
Are picking at the dyke. Weep and you will unmix
The mortar, and the salt black sea will run
And catch and trip and drown us, one by one.
For walls are weaker than their strongest bricks.
Behind our stone, the moon-fed tide expands

To flood our fens. We walk with desperate care,
The locks are fragile and the wind is swelling,
Windows will rattle us awake, eyes wide,
To stare, lying unsurely side by side,
Quiet and fearful; there is no telling
What dreams will flesh out of the noisy air.

The stones had fallen down. We woke too late.
He has unlatched the house, smashed through the pains,
While we slept out our sixth and darkest night,
And taken back his gross seigneurial right.
Today he swills the cultivated plains,
Salting our clay; reclaiming our estate.

Oystermouth Cemetery

Grass lap; the stone keels jar,
scratch quietly in the rippling soil.
The little lettered masts dip slowly
in a little breeze, the anchors here
are very deep among the shells.

Not till the gusty day
when a last angel tramples down
into the mud his dry foot hissing,
down to the clogged forgotten shingle,
till the bay boils and shakes,

Not till that day shall the cords snap
and all the little craft float stray
on unfamiliar tides, to lay their freight
on new warm shores, on those strange islands
where their tropic Easter landfall is.

Third Station

Fall. And between the grey air
and your stone back will run the stream,
quick, cold, of weeping breath,
the mind's sour spit of overnight,
coating the broken skin against its load.

Lift. And between the stone spine
and the sun's weight are caught
the leavings of the mind, the grounds
that cloud the bottom of the heart, and shaken
bitter it, Press to the sun your skin.

Turn. And between the weights of heaven and self
rub small the crying grain and burst
the puckered gelid streams. Wind tight the press
and mill our parching salt, our black and needful flour.
Bread. Tears.

Pantocrator: Daphni [1]

Pillars of dusty air beneath the dome
of golden leaden sky strain to bear up
his sweaty heaviness, his bulging eyes
drawn inwards to their private pain,
his hands arthritic with those inner knots,
his blessings set aside.
He has forgotten us, this one,
and sees a black unvisitable place
where from all ages to all ages he will die
and cry, creating in his blood
congealing galaxies of heat and weight.
Why should he bless or need an open book?
we know the words as well as he,
the names, Alpha, Omega,
fire from fire, we know your cry
out of the dusty golden whirlwind, how you forget
us so that we can be.

[1] The mosaic of Christ the ruler of all in the
monastery of Daphni, Greece.

Augustine

Take off your shoes,
paddle again in the hot dust.
My mother baked me on theses hot stones,
a foreign father handled, pressed
and broke and packed me back
to feed his furnaces
here on the baking dust.

Take down the curtains
round your hot bed.
The long moon shines away
back through the talking hours
of young men's faces damp with eloquence.
the midnight dust under the window
paints me my shadow, light and cold.

Take it and read.
Not now the child's lost voice
climbing the garden wall
in that exact and northern afternoon
to coax me into play. Take up
your shadow, read me
from the bakestone squares.

Take up the stones
and find the choked foundations.
My fingers push the dust away
from broken, staring faces,
half my heart. The world's mosaic
shattered for centuries in the sand
before my memory.

Take up your voice
and tell your shadow's story. If
I weave this web out of my belly,
spread it between the broken ribs
of the hot square, then shall I catch
the winged and stinging visitor,
breaker of each night's sleep?

Take off your shoes.
This dust is mine, this knotted web
is mine, this shadow
is my shape for you, and when
the hot dust scalds your eyes to tears,
who is it weeps with you to soak
your dust to speaking clay?

Indoors

Beaten and close the earth in here,
small blunt old fingers day to day
packing the corners, moulding down serrated tops
along the walls; then pull and plait the springing brambles
into screens and springing grills, a scrollworked coverlet,
Sometimes the spines will catch, lift up a flake of settled skin,
sometimes a drop swells of small thin old blood. Or earth
runs in the cleft of a white hard old scar, mind wanders to
the recollected blow and bleeding, for an hour or two, from
        day to day,
whispering, familiar.

This is the house that years built, dropping soil
from the loose screes. Straddling the hill, the cottage sheds
        its tiles,
the books begin to corrugate with damp. Home
is the cleft where earth runs, and a little old thin blood,
home's where the hurt is, white and familiar as a bone.

Rublev[1]

One day, God walked in, pale from the grey steppe,
slit-eyed against the wind, and stopped,
said, Colour me, breathe your blood into my mouth.

I said, Here is the blood of all our people,
these are their bruises, blue and purple,
gold, brown, and pale green wash of death.

These (god) are the chromatic pains of flesh,
I said, I trust I make you blush,
O I shall stain you with the scars of birth

For ever. I shall root you in the wood,
under the sun shall bake you bread
of beechmast, never let you forth

to the white desert, to the starving sand.
But we shall sit and speak around
one table, share one food, one earth.

---

[1] Andrei Rublev's icon showing the persons of the Trinity as
angels seated at a table dates from the fourteenth century
and is in the Tretyakov Gallery, Moscow.

Snow Fen

On these drum-tight pegged flats, it does not fall
in blankets rucked around the soil,
soft fleece around the raw veins, no,
but drains away the colourblocks
leaving the pool of hollow bone.
It has called back the bleach, the chalk,
the pulse along a whistling buried wire
below the marsh, the monody,
bat-pitched, of the electric stars.

Sketches of street and hedge
and scribbled farms, the pencilled query notes
against the ledger, smear down steadily
to a grey page, rinsed at last
to its sharp grain again;
an unsuccessful cold and clichéd snap
soaks out, the canvas is tacked down
drum-tight and thirsty for the brush
of some less academic sky.

Kettle's Yard [1]

4 March 1984

Pebbles and sea-light,
drift of grain across an ebbing floor,
land's end. The wind is sharp as gulls
past David's Pembroke window,
lettering the stars across
a winter wall.

The gods are grey
and concave, finger-printed into hollow eyes,
their stones warm ash. Fires on the shore
fold when the night drops and we build
the ferns to pack us warm
in crackling beds.

A bell for morning,
pebbles at dawn push damp and black,
teasing awake. The wind is sharp as gulls,
so up the stairs: the sand swells round
a blunted skull. I wash
my face in stone.

---

[1] The unique 'domestic' Cambridge gallery
established by David Jones's friend Jim Ede.

September Birds

Down in the small hollow where the currents shift
slowly, and drop with the thinning sun, the crows
float, crowding the shallow slopes of air,
and vague as specks of stubble fire: the sun
has scattered them from thinning flames, has clapped
a hollow hand, once, twice, a glowing wooden gong,
a log that cracks sharp in the ashes, and
has given wings to the charred dust.
                                    Later, it hangs
moonlike and old with woodsmoke in a black tree
up on the ridge. The crows, snared by the netted oaks,
stick still, the scraps of paper from the fire, yesterday's news
and last week's envelopes. The words come back on them
at sunrise, faintly traced. Sometimes we read
our home addresses.

The White Horse

They guessed, as they dug off the turf,
the sign that waited for them
where the chalk lines fell out,
scattered and compact,
bones for an augury, divining stalks,
the cupped hill's ideogram: *Beast*, it said,
but do not be afraid.
This is no foreign word:
under the swell of dredging labour
it is quick and clear;
the white earth runs like water.

Cornish Waters

Above Boscastle

Grey, warm and stony air
hangs from the clouds in swaying pillars,
and the rain, complex, occasional,
pricks a soft skin.

The green slopes heave
down through the cloud, against the sand,
swallowed and drained off at the bay,
collapsed at journey's end.

Up on the stormy hills
the travellers drop through the grey troughs,
their breath filled up with rain,
eyes under water.

And from the sea,
the level concrete of the sea, who looks,
unmoved and private on the quay
at the land's wrecks?

St Endellion: in church

Between the twinkling granite spars,
the tide is almost at the roof,
pushing the jostling drift of beams.

Lapping insistent words in flood
cajole and smooth Atlantic scarps;
the rock grows deep around the swell.

The little waves will clap their hands,
after the rhythm drops; the stains
paint little transient peaks of dark.

Blackness of words, dense symphonies,
push at the jostling drift of beams
that seal and smooth the granite well.

Dead wood, the drift of nameless craft,
light with the memories of drowning,
hedges the fields of rhythmic dark.

The tide is turning with the roof still dry.

Goonhilly Downs

Wrapped in damp furs, the cold Sidonians
looked in the pits of tin and bought
and hammered out a tongue for awkward contracts,
laying the spiky consonants of Canaan
around the mines, the dangerous dark pools,
where wealth and death, with their loud vowels, hide.

Wedges of thorn, the spiky bone expecting
flesh that will never come, drop a black image
on to the moor's puddles, where the sky,
plain between showers, shines, a thin and equal light;
and in the mirror, the Phoenician consonants
tread back into their distant native text:

Lands before commerce, loss, desire
voiced on the thorn complaints and bargaining;
before the showers come back to dig the moor
with metal hollows mined down to the vein.
A, says the wind, and when the first rain falls,
O, says the scarred pool round its fractured spines.

Camelford (in honour of Regional Water Companies)

Rain is transparent, irresistible,
extravagant and obstinate,
it never will be wooed, to come or go,
like words, or grace.

Rain can be caught, drunk, trapped,
woven with particles of solid dark,
thickened in renal channels, flavoured
with compromising flesh.

Rain must be purchased in a thirsty time
(when knots of charity are dry to breaking point),
clouded and dense with lodging in the guts
of canny men.

Rain sours in the ruts of foresight, payment
salts it to piss, so that it cannot fall
cold on a breaking skin, graceful
for tongue and stomach.

Rain's not exhausted, can't be wooed to go;
the dark still gathers out of which,
heavy and wet as words or grace, it falls
to wash sores; flood banks.

Bach for the Cello

By mathematics we shall come to heaven.
This page the door of God's academy
for the geometer,

Where the pale lines involve a continent,
transcribe the countryside of formal light,
kindle with friction.

Passion will scorch deep in these sharp canals:
under the level moon, desire runs fast,
the flesh aches on its string,
without consummation,

Without loss.

Los Niños [1]

Niño de Vallecas

Look. Big feet and chubby legs
stretched out.
Again. The mouth, lifting a little,
knowingly. I am unhappy; I have noticed
that this is not an accident.
Again. The eyes reach vaguely.
I am unhappy. What will you do?
Are you my friend? What will you give
a child disguised
as a man dressed as a child?

Don Sebastian

What you must do is look me in the eyes
today, the eyes I turned on them, King Philip,
the Infantes, the Inquisitor, the Cardinal my master,
saying, Now, laugh; pity; befriend,
if you so dare. They looked across my head,
friendly and sorry; my ears were close enough
to hear their heaving stomachs' mirth.
So here I sit, stranger, at your eyes for once,
not at your reeking crotch. Now:
pity; befriend. I do not think
I shall be first to drop my gaze, and you may guess
what these cold knuckles hold so close.

Don Pedro

I am the little man
that potent fellows fear
for I run chuckling

between their legs
stealing the privilege
of your stuffed trunks.

Down where you do not come
there lives the world of little folk,
bright, bitter, sniggering
at your swelled dramas. Why?
down here we're hungry:
concentrates the mind.

[1] The sequence is prompted by Velasquez' paintings of the
court dwarves of Phlip IV; from the documentary sources
we know something of their histories and character.

First Thing

The last bit of the dream is letters falling,
soft and regular, the papery flutter
rhythmic on the mat. Not unlike
grey tides licking sand. Waking
is water leaking in; the stuff
out there wobbles and swells
and settles grudgingly into a dryish
daytime shape. And the letters
leaking in resolve themselves
as the dry short breaths
of a nextdoor body, finding
its way out of the night
into slow breakfast time,
the food, the light, a few words,
and the apprehensive, unavoidable
opening of envelopes.

Dream

News of another ceasefire broken: Sarajevo?
somewhere like that. Anger and shame. I stammer
to the person I am drinking with and whom I don't
know very well. I'm crying, quite a lot (I do
in dreams). We are due, next, at a seminar
on violence, held in a courthouse or a theatre,
something like that. What I remember is two speakers,
one cropped and harsh: I find it hard
to formulate my question. One bearded,
articulate and reasonable, talking of victims,
tragedy, the pathos of God trapped in a world
of risks. He sounds like dense stringed music.
It is time to leave, and I fall into step
with him or someone from the benches opposite
(theatre? chapel? parliament?), bearded,
articulate and friendly. We have much in common.
He leads me round behind the theatre
or courthouse; the path narrows between iron railings.
He rounds a corner. There is no one. Stone and iron
closing in. In front of me, a haze of wasps,
alive and dead, some sticking in the dense
and whiteish webbing stuck across the path. I feel
my legs slow down; I know there is no corner
left to turn. I feel the first sting on my right hand
between wrist and thumb. I know I am going to die.

Feofan Grek: the Novgorod Frescoes

Did Yeats mean this?[1] because when sages
stand in the fire, this happens. Skin
umbers and cracks and shines. And then
on hands, shoulders and skirts, the splash
and dribble; you could think the bells have melted
    from their perch,
so that the roaring hollows fall, lazy as snow,
bright liquid pebbles. And then, long
after the eyes have gone, the cheekbones
gleam, razored with little scars in parallel,
the surgery of initiation, letting through
furnaces under the dun hard skin.
We slow down more and more as the heat rises; surfaces
dry up, something inside swells painfully.
The razor makes its first cut. From the oven walls,
out of the searing dusk, they smile
(not at us) blindly.

[1] In his poem 'Sailing to Byzantium'. Feofan Grek's frescoes
of 1378 are in the Cathedral of the Transfiguration in the
ancient city of Novgorod, a hundred miles south of
St Petersburg.

Thomas Merton: Summer 1966 [1]

Bright post-examination weather; in the redundant
classroom, the only point seems here, the belly
of Kentucky heat, the shaven sweating mariners
singing Gregorian shanties in a slow
light evening. What do I want? What sixteen-year-olds want,
no doubt; but also: to learn how to sail that sweaty ship,
words falling moistly from the timber, shining,
Latin, American, French. And the horizon that you think
(so slow the light, so slow the gestures and the voices)
night never quite closes on.

               The same month
you made a landfall, emptied on to the shore,
gasping and heaving against a new hard element,
against the solid sand. And now I read you, years on,
leap and flail, mouth wide, reaching—you once-fluent fellow—
for the words to fix it, finding in the unfixable
a bizarre homeliness. You spent my sixteenth birthday
making a clean(ish) breast of things to the steel smile
of Abbot James. You staged show after show
for friends, then cancelled. Not to make sense is
what most matters.

               What was I seeing,
then, that summer? light from a dead star?
Not quite. But who could tell the night, closing its mouth,
the hard sand, were, after all, where the hot songs
would lead? Practise the Gothic scales for long enough
and they will conjure, surprisingly, this place, flat concrete blocks,
convenience foods, an empty page to look into,
finding the anger; painting, then blotting faces you might wear,
hers, yours, that only in fiction would stand still.
Not to make sense. inside the keel of sweating ribs,
not to make sense but room.

[1] At this time Merton, the radical monastic genius, poet and social critic,
was entangled in a tormenting and unconsummated love affair.

Walsingham: the Holy House

Red kites against a dark blue sky: the flames
beating and clapping round their poise, they fight
wordlessly to hold upright against the draught.

The fat nightlights grow steep, briefly
narrowing their upended eyes, the wavering lines
converge, drop like a plumb, and for a moment

Breath sits upright against the draught, the fat flesh
caught where the beams cross, soundless, perhaps
frightened: fast, without strain, the fire stoops.

Penrhys [1]

The ground falls sharply; into the broken glass,
into the wasted mines, and turds are floating
in the well. Refuse.

May; but the wet, slapping wind is native here,
not fond of holidays. A dour council cleaner,
it lifts discarded

Cartons and condoms and a few stray sheets
of newspaper that the wind sticks
across his face—

The worn sub-Gothic infant, hanging awkwardly
around, glued to a thin mother.
Angelus Novus:

Backing into the granite future, wings spread,
head shaking at the recorded day,
no, he says, refuse,

Not here. Still, the wind drops sharply.
Thin teenage mothers by the bus stop
shake wet hair,

Light cigarettes. One day my bus will come, says one;
they laugh. More use 'n a bloody prince,
says someone else.

The news slips to the ground, the stone dries off,
smoke and steam drift uphill
and tentatively

---

[1] Penrhys is a council estate in the Rhondda Valley, and also
(like Walsingham) the site of a medieval shrine of Our Lady.

Finger the leisure centre's tense walls and stairs.
The babies cry under the sun,
they and the thin girls

Comparing notes, silently, on shared
unwritten stories of the bloody stubbornness
of getting someone born.

Curtains for Bosnia

Not iron but glass; smoother, bewildering.
We couldn't understand why they
Would shake their heads and shrug,
Not understanding, when they looked so near.

And not a curtain but a dome:
Rays from a reasonable sun drawn in,
Bent into thick and beaming probes, to drive
Rational passions deep into the soil,

Where the roots swelled, grew muscular
Grew dense and anxious in the dark,
Began to feel out for a grip to choke
Each other, sent up damp and glaring shoots.

Inexorable soft pressures crack the glass.
Cold; other sounds; then piece by piece,
the shards drop a sky's worth of reasonable light
Slicing the crowded greenery.

Who knows where the sky's needles go,
Whose flesh is cut? But the ground dries,
Under the sun, and the fat roots grow spindly
As old limbs do when there's no more blood to spare.

The devil, said the witches, had an iron prick,
Icecold and smooth. Glass into iron; a reasonable sun,
Nourishing, resolving, folds into a shaft
Of rapists' surgery, till there's no more blood to spare.

So much, we say, for warm and clear illusion,
For the sealed surfaces of thought that incubate
The vegetable nightmares, fright, despair.
Now they can hear the music of our ironies.

Only: now we can hear, wishing
We couldn't understand, they look so near.

Murchison Falls

Physics gets nervous sometimes: can we manage?
can we keep upright on the narrow board of law
in a tight corner with the speed rising?
—so sets itself these adolescent dares: go on,
solve this! Jump; walk the wire; dodge
the zigzagging traffic. Push unlikely bundles
down canals too tight for them, spring them
from world to world, water to air,
and catch them as they drop. Tighten the passageways
so that the pitch goes razor-sharp, and the flow bumps
over more stones along the jostled path
and sounds come thicker. Squeeze, stretch,
strike; and the equations, sweating, give their answers.
Turn up heat and choke the roads: come
to the edge of things and sounds, and look!
says physics, I can do it, I can jump and land,
and leave a map vibrating in the cloud, I move
so fast you must stand still.
                    The mica
shines in the rock as though the spray
has petrified. Physics relaxes as the stone
and water drop to the levels where the idle crocodiles
wait for what physics sends them in crushed parcels
down the chute. The test is passed, the lung
forced open; something has crossed the plaited
crossfire currents to hang steadily in the rapid air
as if said, as if written, once for all.

Kampala; the El Shaddai Coffee Bar

The patron sometimes calls in for a glass,
perhaps; sits with his back
to the door.

Eyes shine and water in the woodsmoke;
who can tell who might be
welcome here?

Woodwind: Kanuga in March

Rain shades in the pines, with steady strokes
and nothing moves. The window is a screen
of drizzling verticals, normality, events,
gameshows and costume drama to be resumed
soonish. On the one tree, the patch of earth red
worries, though; alive? Ready to jump or fly? No. Watch.
Nothing moves. The bloody elbow of a branch
recording some unmanageable load of last month's
snow, a secret life exposed, spicy and naked: life,
but not as we know it, Jim? Ready to move?
the fleshy ochre timber squeezing
into a bird-shaped pellet, climbing the drizzling rods,
it lays a red trail into the wet, grows wooden wings,
hoots like an oboe as the air rushes through
a splintered mouth, moans with the recollection
of the weight that broke it into life,
ready to spring. The air smoothes its grain,
the rain points and polishes its blind head,
slowly soaks it through. The other birds watch carefully.
The moment comes when it stands, still starts falling,
drops fast with the rain, wings folded, and the steady note
climbs into the white, and the claws like a hawk
fall on the gap again at the branch's wounded corner.
The glow returns against the rain, quietly. There is, after all,
no other place to live but on the corner where the cold loads fall.
The cooing instrument rises in panic, squawks and shrills and finds
nothing to say. This is a place where as the rain suggests,
things come home to roost. Although the red eye, the secret flesh,
won't close. I move. Have I seen anything? It winks and preens.
What do we know?

REMEMBERING JERUSALEM

Jerusalem Limestone

I

When you try
to cultivate a plot by the Dead Sea,
you find that pouring on fresh water
brings the salt
nearer the surface.

Up on the hills,
the lurching terraces are full of vines
and olives, and the terraces are rimmed
with stone, white
as a scrubbed doorstep,

White as the scurf
meandering the length of a cold shore
after polluted tides, as if the oil
and wine drained
down at last

Into a thirst
of sand and sea-water, a mouth
at the far edge of words or breath, a face
with salt
breaking the surface

II

And when you see
the staircase hills, white, olive, grey,
the stones hang there like snow
along the edge
of evergreens.

The vines and groves
are posies, stuck by children's hands
into the winter soil, hard
under blankets;
tomorrow dead.

Winter's what lasts.
The oil glow sinking like bonfires
into grey flakes, a twisted log
or two, already
slipping down

Under tonight's
fresh fall; only the cold
can be relied on to come back.
The wine is chilled
long before harvest.

III

When you touch,
your hands will come away dry,
faintly powdered, classroom hands, to rub
back into damp
adhesive life

Up on the hills
the lurching lines cover the board
we can't decode. This is a country
thick with scripts
most won't know.

But the dust
sits in the folds of clothes
and lungs and larynx. What we want
to say explodes
a chalky retching.

Winter.
the dusty coughs like guns,
The class dismissed, untaught.
Something not understood.
The white dry hill.

Gethsemane

Who said that trees grow easily
compared with us? What if the bright
bare load that pushes down on them
insisted that they spread and bowed
and pleated back on themselves and cracked
and hunched? Light dropping like a palm
levelling the ground, backwards and forwards?

Across the valley are the other witnesses
of two millennia, the broad stones
packed by the hand of God, bristling
with little messages to fill the cracks.
As the light falls and flattens what grows
on these hills, the fault lines dart and spread,
there is room to say something, quick and tight.

Into the trees' clefts, then, do we push
our folded words, thick as thumbs?
somewhere inside the ancient bark, a voice
has been before us, pushed the densest word
of all, abba, and left it to be collected by
whoever happens to be passing, bent down
the same way by the hot unreadable palms.

Calvary

The metalled O. Like Bethlehem, like
a baroque drain in the marble floor;
when your hand has been sucked in, it comes away
from its complicity moist,
grimy, sweet-scented.

The Stone of Anointing

All day they oil and polish, rubbing
as if the stone were troubled, rippled with
the angel's windy touch; as if the stone
were sprung like a cramped muscle, and a hard warm hand
could loosen it; as if the hoarse determined breath
and the hot oil could stop the choking, break a seal
on some unseen and frozen lung.
As if they couldn't see themselves. And only when
the stone falls still will their tired polished
faces look back at them; ready to receive
Christ laid on them like a cloth.

Easter Eve: Sepulchre

Constantine knew, of course, just what he wanted:
smooth verticals and marble, crushed glass rolled underfoot,
room for archangels with their orbs and wands,
space for cool power to stroll, relaxed and heavy-footed

Out to the little scented hedges, under a cross that shimmers,
silver and rubies, soft shadows lapping at the ankles.
He cut and smoothed, levelled and piled and spread:
light; crystal; breezy veils; a new, enlightened holy hill.

History (or something) disagreed. The centuries squared up,
exchanged curt, recognizing nods, moved in,
folded and packed, crumpled and stripped and boxed:
the shadows shook themselves, lurched up and smiled

From a new height; people found other things
to do with silver. Air from the marble lungs
is punched out, and the colonnades are crushed and processed
into a maze of ditches, damp stone capsules,

Whorls, cavities, corners with don't-ask smells
and fairground decoration. A collapsing star, screwing its stuff
into the dark: soaring heat, density, a funnel
spinning towards the opposite of anything.

                              * * *

Saturday afternoon, the bodies squashed, wet, boxed,
breathing into the shadows full of smells and tinsel;
flame leaks and spits out of the singularity,
sparks a cracked bell. Iron, rope, smoke

Pant in the tight dark, a light-footed,
high-strung passing. Afterwards we breathe,
dry off the sweat and crying, ask what history
is after, bullying us into waking, into this oppositeness.

Low Sunday: Abu Ghosh

Calm, fluent, the Mass moves
like robes on a walking body, upright
and in no hurry, the chanted French
swings loose between the stresses.

Finding its way in here
something not quite the hard dawn,
crackling out of the grave, but
heavy, lumbering maybe, quiet,

As it pads in from downstairs,
lies down and looks at us, something
idle (maybe), breathing just audibly,
not without noticing; not to be avoided.

GRAVES AND GATES

'. . . that through the grave and gate of death we may
pass to our joyful resurrection'

BOOK OF COMMON PRAYER

Rilke's Last Elegy

Die ewige Strömung
reisse durch beide Bereiche alle Alter
immer mit sich und übertönt sie in beiden

The river flows in both kingdoms. On the side
we don't see, the moon side, it collects the things
we don't see: slivers of ice between the ripples,
and small blue leprosies, and tiny stars that prick
and cut us as we drink; moon-sounds, the anxious hawking
of a fox, the little screams of casual prey, the car-alarm
five silent streets away (you know that if you wake
and look, you'll never find it; it is another kingdom).

So when you whisper into the stream, the words run
round through the moon's valleys, where we don't see,
coming back strange: swollen or scarred, not lining up
and answering. This time round, they prick and scratch
the throat till it flows black, a winter river
fed by the rains we don't see. Bit by bit
the other kingdom spreads, and what we say drowns softly
all sounds smothered. Then the river dries. The earth

Puckers and shrinks, as quiet as the moon. And a few words
lie in their white bed, covenanting stones.

Nietzsche: Twilight

At the clinic, he broke windows, shouting
that there were guns behind them, desperate
not to be shielded by the thin, deceiving skin
that looked as if it wasn't there. He liked
the opaque curtain or the open sky; not this.
His mother took him home; out for walks,
she told him, Put on your nice professor's face,
when they met friends. His head grew vast,
pulling him downwards till he could not breathe.
At night he roared; during the day, My voice
is not nice, he would whisper. White,
swollen, his skull drowned him like a stone,
his breath, at the end, the sound
of footsteps on broken glass.

Simone Weil at Ashford

Upstairs into the air: a young god,
pupils dilated, blows into his little flute.
At each stair's end, he breaks it, reaches for a new one,
climbs again. Below the crowd blurs, hums,
ahead the sky is even, dark from the bare sun.
Breaking the last instrument, he waits,
and in a while they will tear out his heart,
now it is still and simple as the rise and fall
of tides. The crowd and the sun breathe him in.

No, we don't walk like him. We stagger up
the steps in padded jackets, moonboots,
crash-helmets, filters and shades. In gravity.
Some of us try to strip; but what's beneath
is very cold, even under the dark bare sun:
a stiff, gaunt crying, I must not be loved,
and I must not be seen, and if I cannot walk like god,
at least I can be light and hungry, hollowing my guts
till I'm a bone the sentenced god can whistle through.

Tolstoy at Astapovo [1]

Off through the looking-glass he ran:
into the world of hedges, brooks, black and white
    cantonments,
the snapping Queen to urge him on, the fevers
rising and falling, painting black or white
the country of his choices. All around the iron lines
run to a point. Ahead of him strolls Platon,
not looking back; he runs till he is breathless,
burning, but he can't catch him. In the next-door squares
the pieces crowd, the journalists, the relatives, the hopefuls,
the *starets* in the ladies' loo, the script consultants,
newsreel men, police. Check.

Heat and smoke in the little squares; shivering,
he thinks of taking up a long-lost country skill
as quaint as thatching, complicated, unselfconscious,
the sort of thing you pick up in the hours
of glazed winter boredom, the absent-minded endlessness
of a poor childhood. *How do peasants die?*
Some things you can't get into at this age. He knew
he was too old to die, fingers too stiff for plaiting
the spiny ends. He put his head down in the straw.
Mate. All the words came tumbling
backwards out of his dream.

[1] Leo Tolstoy died in the stationmaster's house (now a museum)
in Astapovo (now Tolstoy).

Bereavements

In memory of Jim and Letty Morgan

Beginning with the purchase order:
Notice was served on some years' livelihood
(no choice lucid imperatives drive rapidly;
they need their motorways), and then
the hospital, and notice served on some years' love
(or something like it), confident highspeed
mortality (no choice, not even purchase)
So that he watched the dusty rubbled bed,
those months, the engines ploughing up
                            some years of him,
the furrows slowly merging in the flesh and mud,
the shrinking face, the swelling pools, bewildered,
waiting for clearance. Till the knot was tied,
black gravel rollered down, where the imperatives
run smoothly off for the horizon. In the house,
behind the window she put in out back, he sits
and sees remembered grass still springing underneath
the lucid wheels. He will not go,
not leave the stranded house; his livelihood,
his years, are razored down to this,
                            eyes at this window.
Nowhere else, no choice.

Winterreise: for Gillian Rose, 9 December 1995

Morning

The flat fields tramp towards the Severn.
I know there is no cliff to drop from
at their edge, only the sand and the wet still sheets.

This morning, though, the thick and chest-constricting
light, the level, rose-grey clouds and the remains
of icy fog stand between fields and water,

And the horizon has to be a steep edge, has to be
the cliff where Gloucester fell that never-to-be measured
drop from his body to the ground.

And down, a long way down, below the frost,
must be soft embers sending up the light
from fires the night-fog has muffled but not killed.

Afternoon

Still, where you were concerned, we always
arrived too late; too late, myopic, short of sleep,
with fingers stumbling to decipher messages
you left for us, engraved in a hard surface.
It was a distant relative of yours who drove
his lawyer's reed into the black Sinai basalt
till the calligraphy of little streams broke out
to age the hopeless rock as if with history,
as if with words; another kinsman, distant or not too distant,
writing in falling sweat on stone, body to ground, something
his friends never quite managed to read. Tracing, unthinkingly,
a pattern of spilled wine on the dayroom table,
never quite managing to meet each other's eyes, or not for long,
we test the feel of an unyielding difficulty, not yet sure
of handling this, of finding where the streams combine,
reading what the wet fingertips decode.

Night

Dying by degrees, perhaps, is a winter journey:
connections cancelled unexplained, the staff,
their patience ebbing, closing amenities, one by one, around you.

The temperature falls, and for an hour you sit
on a plastic bench, aching for sleep,
under the surly light that strips you

For some always-delayed inspection; so even,
so hard, that for so long you cannot see the dark:
the homely dark, with its fierce small fires.

Flight Path

For Delphine Williams; August 1999

Dead souls walk straight as Roman legions
from Bredon Hill, striding from fort to fort,
from one sullen, round-shouldered rise
to the next, stopping (perhaps) on each to gape
and swallow and exchange dumb looks, and wait for orders.

The track runs through the solid tribal world:
crosses a motorway at thirty-seven degrees, lays
a cold strip across a sheep's back, slips
between cup and lip, between eye and screen, between
my child's hand and my own, eases between the window and
      the wind.

The Roman road ignores the aboriginals, their maps
and calendars. But we shuffling primitives can't fail to see
this is the occupying power. Sooner or later, we shall have to learn
to shape our mouths, measure our stride like theirs,
and look nowhere but to the next grazed, wind-scrubbed summit.

Ceibr: Cliffs

For Aneurin Williams; September 1999

The quilt of willowherb muffles
the stream before it drops
invisible to the beach;
the moist whisper thinned
in its straight seaward fall,
the shore sound coming back up, dry
as two palms rubbing steadily
close to your ear, or pages
fingered through, or a hand
stroking an unshaved cheek, hard;
or a thick old fabric, tearing
very slowly. Sea on stone
never settles for good if this
is a story of meeting or
an endless creeping scission:
a palmer's kiss, book skimmed
for the familiar quote, touching
the distant face against
hospital pillows, or
slow surgery, faded cloth
pulled and surrendering
every breath unstitching
something. Whatever,
the hoarse bass echo
doesn't change: just the one
voice, touching or tearing.

Windsor Road Chapel

Cinema (Odeon or Capitol) circa 1959:
only no curtains, just an even, tight-pinned bedsheet
of timber, and a blunt, empty cockpit.
Nothing, it says, will come over your shoulder,
no hidden reels, throwing a hazy line

Across the smoke to play the rainbow fish
that slip around, behind, our watered eyes.
This is the board for unexpected news,
a death, a resignation, raw, cold
as the air outside, flat as the turned-down wish.

God, it seems doesn't live in water, glimpse and flash,
mirror and shade, not still until the day's
damp end. The message on the wires
rubs at the skin's impatient folds
in dry, pale itches, drifts of my neighbour's ash.

The most familiar artefact of brass and pine
nags at the memory; you know what's going to fit
the timber cabinet before too long, the drought
that cures the flesh and seals the blood.
Board: gate: departure, says the sign.

Off you go, then, on static-laden floors,
drawn—as we all are —by unwelcome news;
but even now, not able not to pause
and listen for pursuing streams, rolled
shining and stuttering downhill to the exit doors.

Deathship

in memory of R. S. Thomas

The last years, words from a window
smoothing the sea, the iron back and forth
to probe the fugitive wrinkles
carving a path down to the lost gate.

What hid in the pale clefts till now
feels for the light, a soft uncertain
fingering as if through
stone, through furrows of flint.

The tides pressed neat as for an evening out:
time to drag down a black boat from the shed,
off through the gate, to balance
on the slow sea at dark, ready to sail.

The smoke will rise, the cloudy pillar
wavering across the sky's long page.
At dawn, somewhere westward,
the boat flares in a blaze of crying birds.

CELTIA

Gundestrup: The Horned God

You know him. Sitting and sitting,
sitting until the moss grows
over his eyes, until

The stark bone branches
burst through his skull, until
his mouth and hand and gut will

Shape the one round, tense
metal syllable, at which
the beasts stand still

Snouts cocked and hairs on end,
the salmon frozen in mid-leap,
gripped by the unexpected rider's will.

Sit: till you grow hollow,
round as a cauldron, and your mouth
holds the world cocked, dumb and chill,

And from your brow the knitting bones
twist to a forest of hard sounds; among them things
stand still and frightened. Well

You know.

The Sky Falling

'They [the Celtic chiefs] told him that they feared
only one thing, that the sky should fall'

Arrian, *The Expedition of Alexander*

A joke, perhaps? They still
do it, solemnly meeting
the earnest foreigner's enquiry.
Because there could have been,
surely, no terror

For the lime-rinsed and technicolour-
shirted, head-hungry, henpecked
louts who so irritated
dry Caesar in the promise of an end
so brisk and flat

And messy, like flies squashed
between the pages as the book
claps shut; dying of the applause
of heaven and earth when they
join hands

At the show's end. Or maybe,
after all, serious. Think of them
lurching out of the doorway
to breathe, pee, vomit,
packed with booze

Kebabs and mutual admiration,
into the cold; the snow just starting
and the sky slips gently
and piecemeal into the grass
and vanishes,

Fragments of brief intricacy,
like the bard's lovely, hot,
cosseting songs indoors,
the words that freeze great doings
(rapes, wars)

In symmetries and stars; and going
nowhere. The stories sink
into the grass at night,
and the earth sits there,
not applauding,

Spreading an empty palm;
swallowing the sparks of damp
and formal brilliance. Very
quiet.
No joke.

Posidonius and the Druid

Ridges of bone, moulded, you'd think, by awkward thumbs,
freckles, red stubble, and the large pale astigmatic eyes;
the voice hoarse, fluent, not deep.
Well. People come, like you, he says, looking for secrets.
What we learned from Pythagoras. For a consoling echo
of your sweet doctrine from the untouched caves
of us poor primitives. (Leaning to me.) Do you like
what I've to show you? On his open hand
a knife, bone-handled, stained and smooth.
Your logos is a child, he says, chattering to itself
while it plays on the sand. I am a swimmer.
I am a salmon and a seal. My streams
are made of many fluids, dark swaying planes
on which I travel still as sleep; or where
I leap like silver. The sea. Rain on the skin,
and sweat. Tears and the river over stones.
My blood and yours: the tide that beats below the skin
or in the pulsing from the severed vein,
or from my organ, or from yours, or else the urine
from the hanged man, jerking among the leaves,
whose motions speak to me. Over these waves
I learn to skim my hands, and in these wells
my tongue explores, drinks words.

                                    I take the knife;
like rubbing fingers on a worn inscription,
read it. In my mind, briefly: flat plains,
a straight road running to the edge of things, drab
unfamiliar carts packed close with silent people,
knowing and not knowing what this journey is
on which they're sent by blood and wisdom and
dark quiet waters, and I reach out breathless for the shore,
children and sand, the noise and the unsafety,
drift, spars and groundlessness, but still the anchorage
proper to talking beings.

Altar to the Mothers

Soft-cheeked and honey-breasted,
fruit tumbling at their feet like children, and
semantically-loaded sheaves of corn,
beautiful, terrible; warm thighs and mysteries
and a calm dark regard out of their timeless eyes . . .

Actually no (if this is really them):
they stand in solid sexless line,
headscarved and overcoated, waiting for a bus
to Ebbw Vale or Rotherham; bleak damp endurance of
the never-up-to-standard world.

Men (rightly) shivering laid oil and wine
and sacrificed new shoes, pubertal hair,
unsatisfactory girlfriends, self-respect,
nodding in desperation at the granite words
you can't switch off. No, you do what *you* want, love,

Don't think of me. We've always done what seemed the
        right thing
for you, pet. If you don't respect
yourself, no-one will do it for you. If you've got
your health, there's nothing you can't cope with. What time
do you call this? Why aren't you eating?

You do what you want, love. Divinity is manifest
in the sublime command. Ignore this order; making sure
that you won't, ever. Refused, victorious, inexpugnable,
they settle back, having secured that there will never be
an up-to-standard offering, a world

Free to leave home, to call time what we like.

TRANSLATIONS

Experiencing Death

Don't know a thing about this trip we're going on; they don't
give much away about it. So we don't know where to stand
to look at the unwelcome destination, how to see our death.
Amazed? entranced? or loathing? How the tragic mask twists
    things

Out of an honest shape! But still, the world can give
you quite a cast-list to choose from. Just don't
forget; as long as it's the audience's reaction
that worries you, death's at your elbow on the boards.

No audience fancies corpses. Only when *you* went offstage,
the flats you slipped through let in something else,
a streak of truth: the colour of real foliage
under real sunshine in a real woodland.

For us, the show must go on. All those lines
we learned, struggling and panicky, the stagey gestures
ordered by some director we can't put a face to . . . and then you,
struck off the list, you who are real now a long way off,

Your far-off thereness sometimes overtakes us still, falling
around us like that streak of daylight green, and then
we find, just for a bit, we can play life, not scripts;
not give a damn about applause.

Rilke

95

Roundabout, Jardin du Luxembourg

Out of that foreign land, the gaudy horses
bounce with conviction for a while (never mind
the shadows from the canopy) — the foreign land
that hangs around long enough after closing time before
    it fades.

They all look feisty enough, even the ones
(quite a few) with carts hitched on. Oh look!
A big bad lion seems to have got in. Oh look!
A sweet baby white elephant. What next?

Oh look! A stag, just like the ones you see
out in the woods, except of course this one
happens to have a little girl in blue
strapped in a saddle,

               and the big bad lion's
carrying a little boy in white, who's hanging on
for dear life, while the lion grins and slobbers—
Look! the sweet baby white elephant again . . .

Those girls are getting too big for the ride,
but there they go, giggling and darting sparky looks
all over the place in mid-flight, and they—oh,
there's the sweet
             baby
                 white . . .

Round and round and round and round and round.
Red. Green. Grey. Red. Aching to stop.
Nowhere to go. The little profiles sketchy, hardly started.
Listen! There's someone laughing as they spin,
as if they were —well, happy, blissful even;
wasting their breath, casting a shimmer round
this blind asthmatic game.

Rilke

Angel

He bends his head away, says his hard No to everything
that might commit him, tie him down,
because there's always something circling, always
just about to land, something enormous
pushing up through his heart.

      And the deep blackness
of the sky is full, for him, of shapes,
and any one of them could summon him—come here!
see this! So for God's sake, don't try to put
what weighs *you* down into those airy hands of his;
because it's you they'd grab for.

      In the middle of the night
they'd burrow in and scrabble like a maniac
round your house, and clutch you, wrestle you to the floor,
squeezing and kneading, wanting to sculpt and hollow,
to push you, break you out of the form you know
        that clothes you round.

Rilke

Hymn for the Mercy Seat

Wonder is what the angels' eyes hold, wonder:
The eyes of faith, too, unbelieving in the strangeness,
Looking on him who makes all being gift,
Whose overflowing holds, sustains,
Who sets what is in shape,
Here in the cradle, swaddled, homeless,
And here adored by the bright eyes of angels,
The great Lord recognised.

Sinai ablaze, the black pall rising,
Through it the horn's pitch, high, intolerable,
And I, I step across the mortal frontier
Into the feast safe in my Christ from slaughter.
Beyond that boundary all loss is mended,
The wilderness is filled, for he,
Broker between the litigants, stands in the breach,
Offers himself for peace.

Between the butchered thieves, the mercy seat, the healing,
The place for him to test death's costs,
Who powers his very killers' arms,
Drives in the nails that hold him, while he pays
The debt of brands torn from the bonfire,
Dues to his Father's law, the flames of justice
Bright for forgiveness now, administering
Liberty's contract.

Soul, look. This is the place where all kings' monarch
Rested a corpse, the maker of our rest, and in
His stillness all things always move,
Within his buried silence.
Song for the lost, and life; wonder
For angels' straining eyes, God's flesh.
They praise together, they adore,
'To him', they shout, 'only to him'.

And I, while there is breath left to me,
Say, Thanksgiving, with a hundred thousand words,
Thanksgiving: that there is a God to worship,
There is an everlasting matter for my singing;
Who with the worst of us, in what
He shares with me, cried under tempting,
A child and powerless, the boundless
Living true God,

Flesh rots: instead, aflame, along with heaven's singers,
I shall pierce through the veil, into the land
Of infinite astonishment, the land
Of what was done at Calvary;
I shall look on what never can be seen, and still
Shall live, look on the one who died and who still lives
And shall; look in eternal jointure and communion,
Not to be parted.

I shall live up the name that God
Sets out to be a mercy seat, a healing, and the veils,
And the imaginings and shrouds have gone, because
My soul stands now, his finished likeness,
Admitted now to share his secret, that his blood and hurt
Showed once, now I shall kiss the Son
And never turn away again. And never
Turn away.

From the Welsh of Ann Griffiths

I Saw him Standing

Under the dark trees, there he stands,
there he stands; shall he not draw my eyes?
I thought I knew a little
how he compels, beyond all things, but now
he stands there in the shadows. It will be
Oh, such a daybreak, such bright morning,
when I shall wake to see him
as he is.

He is called Rose of Sharon, for his skin
is clear, his skin is flushed with blood,
his body lovely and exact; how he compels
beyond ten thousand rivals. There he stands,
my friend, the friend of guilt and helplessness,
to steer my hollow body
over the sea.

The earth is full of masks and fetishes,
what is there here for me? are these like him?
Keep company with him and you will know:
no kin, no likeness to those empty eyes.
He is a stranger to them all, great Jesus.
What is there here for me? I know
what I have longed for. Him to hold
me always.

From the Welsh of Ann Griffiths

Strata Florida

Wind murmurs in the trees at Ystrad Fflur
but does not wake
the dozen abbots dozing in their tombs
while the leaves shake.

Dead with his clever verses, Dafydd too
lies in his bed
Among forgotten warlords, swords dulled,
armour shed.

Summer will come and rouse the wind-stripped trees.
But not the men.
Stones unobtrusively decay. They will not
stand again.

Defeat oblivion rotting monuments
of dead belief.
Why is it then I find no words, here, quietly,
for private grief?

From the Welsh of T. Gwynn Jones

Song for a Bomb

I split and scatter him who splits and scatters,
And in my falling there is Adam's Fall.
Where in this vacuum will you find purpose,
Where in this pattern where a purpose dwells?

It only takes the naked brain to think me,
It only takes a human hand to shape,
And youthful nimbleness to bring to action.
What are you waiting for? Create.

My master quietly pursues his business,
Patient untying of the knotted heart.
Till, fearfully and wonderfully crafted,
Last of his servants forth I come to wait.

My master is the worm that gnaws the root,
My master is the canker in the tree.
But I shall tidy him way for ever
On to the bonfire of death's ecstasy.

From the Welsh of Waldo Williams

In the Days of Caesar

In the days of Caesar, when his subjects went to be reckoned,
there was a poem made, too dark for him (naive with power)
    to read.
It was a bunch of shepherds who discovered
in Bethlehem of Judah, the great music beyond reason and
    reckoning:
shepherds, the sort of folk who leave the ninety-nine behind
so as to bring the stray back home, they heard it clear,
the subtle assonances of the day, dawning toward cock-crow,
the birthday of the Lamb of God, shepherd of mortals.

Well, little people, and my little nation, can you see
the secret buried in you, that no Caesar ever captures in his
    lists?
Will not the shepherd come to fetch us in our desert,
gathering us in to give us birth again, weaving us into one
in a song heard in the sky over Bethlehem?
He seeks us out as wordhoard for his workmanship, the
    laureate of heaven

From the Welsh of Waldo Williams

After Silent Centuries

For the Catholic martyrs of Wales

The centuries of silence gone, now let me weave a celebration;
Because the heart of faith is one, the moment glows in which
Souls recognise each other, one with the great tree's kernel at
    the root of things.

They are at one with the light, where peace masses and gathers
In the infinities above my head; and where the sky moves into
    the night,
Then each one is a spyhole for my darkened eyes, lifting the veil.

John Roberts, Trawsfynydd: a pauper's priest,
Breaking Bread for the journey when the plague weighed on
    them,
Knowing the power of darkness on its way to break, crumble,
    his flesh.

John Owen, carpenter: so many hiding places
Made by his tireless hands for old communion's sake,
So that the joists are not undone, the beam pulled from the roof.

Richard Gwyn: smiling at what he saw in their faces, said,
'I've only sixpence for your fine'—pleading his Master's case,
His charges (for his life) were cheap as that.

Oh, they ran swift and light. How can we weigh them,
    measure them,
The muster of their troops, looking down into damnation?
Nothing, I know, can scatter those bound by the paying of one
    price,

The final silent tariff. World given in exchange for world,
The far frontiers of agony to buy the Spirit's leadership,
The flower paid over for the root, the dying grain to be his cradle.

Their guts wrenched out after the trip to torment on the hurdle,
And before the last gasp when the ladder stood in front of them
For the souls to mount, up to the wide tomorrow of their dear
    Lord's Golgotha.

You'd have to tell a tale of them, a great, a memorable tale,
If only, Welshmen, you were, after all, a people.

From the Welsh of Waldo Williams

Die Bibelforscher

For the Protestant martyrs of the Third Reich

Earth is a hard text to read; but the king
has put his message in our hands, for us to carry
sweating, whether the trumpets of his court
sound near or far. So for these men:
they were the bearers of the royal writ,
clinging to it through spite and hurts and wounding.

The earth's round fullness is not like a parable, where meaning
breaks through, a flash of lightning, in the humid, heavy dusk;
imagination will not conjure into flesh the depths
of fire and crystal sealed under castle walls of wax, but still
they keep their witness pure in Buchenwald,
pure in the crucible of hate penning them in.

They closed their eyes to doors that might have opened
if they had put their names to words of cowardice;
they took their stand, backs to the wall, face to face with
        savagery,
and died there, with their filth and piss flowing together,
arriving at the gates of heaven,
their fists still clenched on what the king had written.

Earth is a hard text to read. But what we can be certain of
is that screaming mob is insubstantial mist;
in the clear sky, the thundering assertions fade to nothing.
There the Lamb's song is sung, and what it celebrates
is the apocalypse of a glory
pain lays bare.

From the Welsh of Waldo Williams

Between Two Fields

These two fields a green sea-shore, the tide spilling
radiance across them, and who knows
where such waters rise? And I'd had years
in a dark land, looking: where did it, where did he
come from then? Only he'd been there
all along. Who though? who
was this marksman loosing off bolts
of sudden light? One and the same the lightning
hunter across the field, the hand to tilt
and spill the sea, who from the vaults
above the bright-voiced whistlers, the keen darting plovers,
brought down on me such quiet, such

Quiet: enough to rouse me. Up to that day
nothing had worked but the hot sun to get me going,
stir up drowsy warm verses: like blossom
on gorse that crackles in the ditches, or
like the army of dozy rushes, dreaming
of clear summer sky. But now: imagination
shakes off the night. Someone is shouting
(who?), Stand up and walk. Dance. Look.
Here is the world entire. And in the middle
of all the words, who is hiding? Like this
is how it was. There on the shores of light
between these fields, under these clouds.

Clouds: big clouds, pilgrims, refugees,
red with the evening sun of a November storm.
Down where the fields divide, and ash and maple
cluster, the wind's sound, the sound of the deep,
is an abyss of silence. So who was it stood
there in the middle of this shameless glory, who
stood holding it all? Of every witness witness,
the memory of every memory, the life
of every life? who with a quiet word

calms the red storms of self, till all
the labours of the whole wide world
fold up into this silence.

And on the silent sea-floor of these fields,
his people stroll. Somewhere between them,
through them, around them, there is a new voice
rising and spilling from its hiding place
to hold them, a new voice, call it the poet's
as it was for some of us, the little group
who'd been all day mounting assault
against the harvest with our forks, dragging
the roof-thatch over the heavy meadow. So near,
we came so near then to each other, the quiet huntsman
spreading his net around us.
Listen! you can
just catch his whistling, hear it?

Whistling, across the centuries of blood
on the grass, and the hard light of pain; whistling
only your heart hears. Who was it then, for God's sake?
mocking our boasts, tracking our every trail and slipping
past
all our recruiting sergeants? Don't you know?
says the whistling, Don't you remember?
don't you recognise? it says; until we do.
And then, our ice age over, think of the force
of hearts released, springing together, think
of the fountains breaking out, reaching up
after the sky, and falling back, showers
of falling leaves, waters of autumn.

Think every day, under the sun,
under these clouds, think every night of this,
with every cell of your mind's branching swelling shoots;
but with the quiet, the same quiet, the steady breath,
the steady gaze across the two fields, holding still
the vision: fair fields full of folk;

for it will come, dawn of his longed-for coming,
and what a dawn to long for. He will arrive, the outlaw,
the huntsman, the lost heir making good his claim
to no-man's land. the exiled king
is coming home one day; the rushes sweep aside
to let him through.

From the Welsh of Waldo Williams

Angharad

All night and every night, she shares her bed
with jostling anxieties, jostling celebrations;
the pains keep her awake, so do the party noises,
all of them welcomed and nursed in her heart's deep seas,
the soil round her doors churned up by the distressed,
the fragile, who know their way infallibly into her courts.
All that she does weaves her a gown to wear,
bright scarlet, running down to cover every inch.

Carrying the chaos of those so breakable hearts,
binding her strength in with theirs to face out the terrors;
the blue crystal dawn of the Kingdom's day
sits on her lap, her own bright daylight,
level and simple, pouring the hospitable wine,
wine for the King's feast, wine for the wound's sting.
Light turns towards light; searching for his clear sun,
she moulds afresh in praise the early-morning unspoilt
    world.
The sun's sister and the four winds' sister and the sister
for days when the waves are bitter and passionate,
and sister too of the anxious watchful star
and its insistent oversight calling us forward.

Fruits from her tree she uses to calm and mend
what anger shatters or jealousy, hands smoothing
wide, unconfined, the gift indifferent to frontiers.
And that no less frontierless ancient agony becomes
longing that tells us plainly where its roots lie
deep in the soil, deep in a black earth.
So what she gives God, she gives from earth's two faces,
the pain, the festival; the tense surprise of sound and metre
    knitting.
And then is what she gives to us, clear under God's sky—
The priesthood of her caring.

From the Welsh of Waldo Williams